The Art of Making Relationships

The Art of Making Relationships

✦

Win the World by Using Relationship-Building Techniques

Saha Nathan B.E, M.B.A

iUniverse, Inc.
New York Lincoln Shanghai

The Art of Making Relationships
Win the World by Using Relationship-Building Techniques

iUniverse books may be ordered through booksellers or by contacting:

iUniverse
2021 Pine Lake Road, Suite 100
Lincoln, NE 68512
www.iuniverse.com
1-800-Authors (1-800-288-4677)

ISBN-13: 978-0-595-35449-8 (pbk)
ISBN-13: 978-0-595-79943-5 (ebk)
ISBN-10: 0-595-35449-1 (pbk)
ISBN-10: 0-595-79943-4 (ebk)

Printed in the United States of America

Contents

Acknowledgements

As with any major building project, it takes a great team to make all of the elements come together. From the bottom of my heart I want to extend my sincerest thanks to:

- **Lena Temilvanan**: Without your encouragement, this book would not have been possible. Thank you for inspiring to write about the art of relationships.

- **Darren Heppner**: I never forget your support and encouragement.

- **Mark and Vivi**: Your unconditional love encompassed me whenever needed, especially through meditation.

- **Rani and Poorna**: For your unwavering enthusiasm, comfort and encouragement.

- **Maharishi Mahesh Yogi**: For teaching us what really matters in life. Meditation made us strong and balanced.

- **Wes Bafus and Miguel Rivera**: Thank you for being a great supporters.

- **Sai Nidamarti**: I never forget your encouragement and helping tendency.

- **Megan Miller and Terri Sontag**: Thanks for bridging and pointing wherever it was needed.

- **My Publisher**: Thanks to Jon and the iuniverse team.

- **To my family:** You love me the most and support me in all my endeavors.

- **To my friends:** I'd have to write a book to mention everybody-thank you very much for evaluating this, as for your acceptance.

Introduction

It is a common misconception that our relationships either succeed or fail due to mysterious circumstances beyond our control, such as being "right" for one another or being lucky enough to be blessed with the certain type of magic or chemistry best friends or perfect couples appear to possess. This myth is perpetuated by the media and by people who have limited understanding as to why some relationships work when others do not.

In this book, you will discover that your encounters all have the potential to evolve into relationships once you understand that forging relationships is an art.

If you have the willingness to learn how to master this art and incorporate meditation into your life, you can deconstruct the mystery and put the power of your destiny back in your control.

PART I
INITIATION

1

What is a relationship?

A relationship is the complete synchronization between two people where a true bond forms and deep intimacy can be experienced. At its core, it is a physical, emotional, energetic harmony. Whether two people are as near as total intimacy requires or a thousand miles apart, this harmony transcends.

This harmony describes any kind of relationship; that of lovers, friends, family; the relationship between co-workers, employees, bosses, customers, clients, patients; the relationship between a person and the Divine; the relationship between you and the store sales person; the relationship between you and your manager; the relationship between you and your environment; the relationship between you and an occasion; the relationship between groups, religions, races, nations; the relationship between all the different people and groups.

There are two kinds of relationships:

1. The first type of relationship, the problem relationship, exhibits a clash of wills. The underlying issue in this relationship is the individual ego. It is difficult to be loved or give love because loving means one has to adjust or give up a part of his or her ego. By feeling the need to deny or change a part of who we are, feelings of panic, untruth and hatred result.

2. The second type of relationship, that of nondiscriminatory, unconditional love, brings compassion, compromise, and sympathy. A true relationship means that there is no physical and emotional struggle between egos. Two bodies exist separately, but their beings have mingled. There is no limit and there is no partition.

Everything we put into our relationship harmony either supports, develops, builds, strengthens, or, conversely, weakens it with tension and distress. Every action a person takes or does not take, everything a person says or does not say, impacts the weather of the relationship's harmony. If we do not pay attention to the harmony between us, small and big distresses will build up in our relationship environment. It is not so much that someone intends to pollute the harmony, but more that he or she either doesn't think about the impact the behavior has on the other person or on the relationship itself. Sometimes people contribute to the distress by trying to protect themselves or get their needs met, which is often, inadvertently, at the expense of the other person.

All relationships have the potential to evolve into love when freed from the selfishness of the ego. Each relationship is a means towards forwarding our life's purpose. Relationships are opportunities to merge our wills with the will of another, thereby creating a greater reality. It is natural that we support, inspire and affirm each other. Mutual love and respect are the basis of all conscious relationships. The deeper we know each other, the more we want to be together.

In reality, we are never hurt by the other, but only by our own fears, attachments, needs and expectations.

The good news is that we each have the power, at any time, to begin to shift our relationship's environment. We can create a relationship of respect, integrity, compassion and justice. We can find love in the deepest sense of the word.

2

We must start by loving ourselves

Do you know that you are beautiful and lovable, just the way you are?
Do your loved ones know your real inner beauty?
Do you follow assertive techniques?
Do people respect you for who you are?
Do you find yourself surrounded by people who appreciate you?

If you can answer "yes" to all of these questions, you are much more likely to construct successful relationships. In creating healthy, loving relationships with others, we need to believe in and love ourselves, as well as be able to recognize our personal weaknesses that we are uncomfortable with because anything we refuse to acknowledge creates an imbalance. Your comfort with yourself allows others to feel comfortable with you. Because the nature of life is to seek stability and integration, any imbalances will be like the recognizable high-pitched wheel, acting out in even more extreme ways to get us to pay attention to an inner need for healing. Moreover, if we cannot love ourselves, we will look for someone else to love us in the hopes they can give us enough love to mask or erase our unlovable characteristics. Unfortunately, in this situation, we tend to attract others who do not love and accept themselves either, thus setting ourselves up for even more hurt and disappointment. Let us talk about how we can learn to love ourselves unconditionally, and see what a wonderful effect that can have in creating healthier relationships in all aspects of our lives.

Many of us have a mental threat: our inner enemy. This inner enemy seems to delight in throwing negative feelings or messages at us, most of which come from painful times in our past, and these messages are continuous. Whenever a positive experience occurs, the enemy escalates and starts criticizing us. This inner enemy must be dismantled because our thoughts are creative and powerful. We literally become what we think, and we do not want to become our own enemy. The inner enemy can be more damaging than any external, real-world obstacle. In relationships, the inner enemy will tell you that you don't deserve or cannot attract a healthier relationship.

If you are with someone who constantly criticizes and disparages you, you can be sure that you constantly criticize and belittle yourself. If you are with someone who is always angry or fearful, it is a reflection of how you feel inside.

We must understand that the people around us have come into our lives to teach us about ourselves. The people we like reflect the loving aspect of ourselves. The people we do not like also reflect the things we do not like about ourselves. We usually get angry and blame them for being wrong. However, instead of blame, try to see the lesson that you need to learn from that person. Once you learn the lesson and are willing to change, the people in your life will either treat you differently or leave your life. In short, if you learn the lessons, you can move on to happier experiences. And if you don't, you can be sure that these same people will keep reappearing in your life until you do.

Sometimes we may become attracted to people who do not encourage our talents and abilities. We try to impress them, but they never really see us or try to spend time to understand us. The problem does not lie in the other, however, but in our own perception. Others' appreciation is merely a reflection of how we see ourselves. If we understand this nature, not surprisingly, that critical, unappreciative character soon disappears from our life.

Try this experiment on yourself, using an open mind and heart: think of someone in your life who irritates you. Now, write down the things you dislike about him or her. Next, sit quietly and think honestly about yourself: when do you do the same things? For example, if the trait you find irritating is criticism, notice where you, too, may be critical of yourself or others. Once you are able to recognize the shortcomings in yourself that you dislike in others, begin to affirm, "I am willing to release the need to be critical of myself and others." Say it over and over again any time you feel like criticizing.

As you do this, you will begin to notice how many times per day you think critical thoughts. Of course this is nothing to criticize yourself for! Just notice and learn. If your pattern is complaining, or assuming failure, or being fearful, adjust the affirmation accordingly. Each time you see that pattern appearing say, "I am willing to release the need to complain, or be fearful, etc." Try to realize that the negative feelings you have created about yourself have merely come from a thought and that a thought can be changed. That is where our freedom and our power lies.

If we continually blame someone else and think they are the problem, we give away our own power. But if you begin to realize that *your thoughts* are the problem, you can take charge, change your thoughts, and move on to the wonderful new experiences that you deserve.

To love ourselves we need to be aware and willing to change for the better:

Stop all criticism: Criticism never changes anything. Refuse to criticize yourself. Accept yourself exactly as you are. Everybody changes. When you criticize yourself, your changes are negative. When you approve of yourself, your changes are positive.

Do not panic yourself: Stop frightening yourself with your thoughts. It is a dreadful way to live. Find a mental image that gives you pleasure (anything like flowers, your god or something else), and immediately switch your frightening thought to a pleasurable thought.

Self-talk: Whenever a problem presents itself, remember to say things to yourself like, "this is only a situation given to me." Remember that nothing will happen if you allow yourself to feel hopeless or depressed.

Be gentle, kind and patient with yourself: As you learn new ways of thinking, treat yourself as you would someone you love. It can be difficult to train yourself to think differently, give yourself time.

Be kind to your mind: Self-hatred only makes you hate your own thoughts. Do not hate yourself for having thoughts. Gently change the thoughts.

Praise yourself: Criticism breaks the inner spirit. Praise builds it up. Praise yourself as much as you can. Tell yourself how well you are doing with every little thing.

Create a support network: Reach out to friends and allow them to help you. You are being strong by asking for help when you need it.

Take care of your body: Learn about nutrition. What kind of fuel does your body need to have optimum energy and vitality? Learn about exercise. What kind of exercise would you enjoy? Cherish and revere the temple that is your body.

Use your mirror: Look into your own eyes often. Express the growing sense of love you have for yourself. Forgive yourself when looking into the mirror.

Set goals: Take a notebook and write down your goals. Look at them every morning as soon as you get out of bed. Close your eyes and visualize your goals throughout the day, and reevaluate your success in achieving them.

Live naturally: Live each and every moment. Be full of interest in the world and create your own environment within it. When I say "live" it does not just mean living with people. It includes living in harmony with nature.

Accept the changes: Today's Saha will not be the same as tomorrow's Saha. Our body changes daily. Our thought process changes and everything else changes daily, too.

Meditate: Practice meditation to understand your mind, body, nature and nature's potential.

Love yourself: Brighten the world with your loving nature and make your surroundings lively.

3

The art of making a relationship

You can win anybody's heart if you understand the art of making a relationship. God created human beings to build harmonious relationships. The moment you harmonize with someone, life becomes a part of paradise.

Harmony is "inter-dependency." This can happen between any two people without expecting anything from each other. People can truly harmonize when they allow themselves to connect and understand the other's perspective.

- **Whatever the relationship in this world, it should not be an arrangement.**
- **Whatever the relationship in this world, it should not come with compulsion.**

The moment you start showing your unconditional love to somebody, you will easily get into that person's heart. The key to unconditional love is not expecting anything in return. The moment you start expecting something from the other person, it is no longer a real relationship.

Many people in this world manipulate relationships like politics, meaning that they are doing something with an expectation. You will not achieve a long lasting relationship in this way. If you start expecting something from your friend or partner, the relationship becomes a business.

When either person is not getting what he/she wants or needs out of the relationship, frustration sets in. Once frustration begins, then people become agitated and that agitation will make you to do anything to achieve your desires. In the end, you will not achieve anything; instead you will lose that person. You do have to be fair to yourself and ensure you are getting what you want out of the relationship, but this bring us back to balance. An equal give and take is imperative to ensure neither party is taking advantage of the other.

A pathway to long lasting relationships:

- The first qualification for long lasting relationship is to take your ego out of the equation.

- Always show your enthusiasm when you move in with a friend/partner. That means you make them feel like they are very important to you.

- Whether it is good or bad, listen to your friend/partner whenever he or she wants to share feelings with you.

- It is important to be a medium through which your friend/partner can release stress. This is especially important when he or she faces any crunch situation.

- A relationship is a process in which we must have patience before it reaches its maturity level. At times (particularly the early stages in a relationship) others may not be willing to listen to you and they may not understand you, but you can help them understand by openly communicating and allowing them to become comfortable with you. This takes time.

- Involve your friends in your life and allow them to contribute to your new ideas and new ventures. This will make them feel connected to you.

- Problems can be used as learning tools because you gain an understanding of the real nature of a friend during a conflict. At the same time, never keep quiet in a conflict situation. Keep on putting your suggestions forth in a calm and comforting manner if you feel you are right. If the problem still persists in the relationship, please give the relationship some space (one day to one week).

4

Communication is the key for any relationship

Communication is an art. If you know how to communicate well, then you can conquer the world. **Good communication is the cornerstone of happy relationships. Learn how to talk and listen successfully.**

Communication undoubtedly plays a foundational role in the development of any healthy relationship. Good communication can help prevent misunderstandings. It also helps solidify a mutual sense of commitment. Indeed, communication plays a critical role in all phases of interpersonal relations, from inception to maintenance. There are ways to communicate with people effectively, and that communication has to have a planned format. This can help two people to communicate in a more healthy and constructive manner.

Communication Barriers:

- Problems arise through arguing, blaming, egoistical talk, not listening properly, and by changing the subject. It is very difficult to resolve any conflict with these barriers. Eventually the end result will be an unhappy relationship or a break up.

- If you consistently talk about yourself, the other person will feel pushed out. Break the habit by asking more questions about the other person.

- If your body language is closed, people will feel rejected. Break the habit by deliberately uncrossing your arms and legs, and smiling more.

- If you keep interrupting, they will feel unheard. Break the habit by learning their verbal and non-verbal signals.

- Communication is ineffective when either person is irritated.

Give attention:

Listening is every bit as important in good communication as making yourself understood. Active listening, as the name suggests, requires active participation. The listener's job is purely to listen, without interruption. In active listening:

- Try to give your full attention to your friend or partner, even if you don't agree with what is being said. Pay attention and listen to his or her point of view. When you are listening, aim to make your friend or partner the center of attention. Always try to see him or her eye to eye, and put all your other thoughts aside until he or she is finished speaking.

- Summarize and clarify with your friend or partner to make sure that you have understood properly. Not summarizing is often worse than not listening at all, because it comes across as if you're not interested.

- Use positive body language, such as a nod or smile, to acknowledge the other person. They will feel more appreciated and will, therefore, be more likely to listen to you.

- Know which questions to ask; it will help you get the right answers. Think about what you're trying to understand about the other, and avoid the guessing games.

- Use silence confidently as a tool to encourage hesitant speakers.

- Think about the words that you hear, not the person saying them.
- Keep an open mind about what people say.
- Formulating a response in your head when someone is speaking is NOT active listening. Wait for a break in the conversation.

To successfully communicate your thoughts, there are many ways to become more effective:

Know how to ask questions:

- Ask a specific question if you want to hear a specific answer.
- Use open-ended questions to gain insight into the other person's character and to invite a response.
- Think about your questions before you start talking.
- Do not be afraid to pause if you need clarification.
- Speak in as natural a tone as possible to create a warm environment.

Know how to talk:

Talk clearly, firmly, and confidently. Always notice his or her body language to find out whether the other person is still involved in what you're saying. Make sure that they do not get distracted. If you're talking about something emotional or intimate that might cause stress to the other person, cut out distractions such as children or a family problem. Then move in close and touch if that is within the boundaries of that relationship. They will relax and be more able to interact with you.

Know how to write:

- Visualize the reader when you are writing a letter or report.

- Avoid using complicated and unusual words or abstract terms. They may obscure your meaning.

- Order your thoughts; even make notes before you start writing a letter.

- Use language appropriate for the writing purpose.

- Consider the multiple meanings language can have when unaccompanied by body language and voice inflection.

Focus on the subject:

Be open and willing to focus on the topic at hand, even if you are a person who can get easily distracted by the external environment. Choose a calm place with few distractions. Sometimes you may fail to focus on the subject. If your friend or partner is not willing to listen you, be patient and keep trying. Show him or her just how loved you feel when they maintain eye contact as you talk, respond to what you say, and ask questions. Tell others when their good listening gets a particularly good result, when it helps you make the right decision or when it makes you feel more positive about a situation.

Timing and presence of mind

For good communication to occur, it must be the right time and place. If either of you is too upset or distracted, the interaction will most likely end up with one of the previously discussed four communication blocks impeding the discussion.

If you know you or your partner is too upset to have a constructive conversation, do the following:

- Stop and cool down. Leave the situation for a while if necessary.

- Set up a specific time and place to talk again.

- Don't interrupt others-they need to have a chance to express themselves.

- Acknowledge your partner's concerns.

- Discuss your feelings in a responsible way.

- If you discuss your partner's behavior, do so in terms of *your* feelings.

- Tell your partner how his or her behavior affects you.

- Let your partner know your feelings when he or she engages in the behavior.

- If all else fails, try to postpone the discussion until later or even the next day. Wait until you can communicate calmly, lovingly and with all the time in the world.

5

Beyond communication

While communication is key to any relationship, there are other aspects that need attention as well. The following five points must also be taken into consideration:

Criticism:

Whenever we criticize someone, we inhibit our ability to take a clear look at the situation. Criticism is very harmful because whenever we call someone egotistical or useless, for example, we start seeing that person as arrogant or useless. Our mind unconsciously keeps on picking up and finding those negative traits in that person. Thus, we become unable to deal with that person as a unique individual.

Stay away from criticizing others. Learn to appreciate and compliment others. Appreciation and compliments have tremendous positive power. They should, however, be genuine.

Understand and accept others:

Understand needs such as affection, love, approval, freedom, respect, and unity. Do not speak to other people about your loved one, but talk to him or her directly to resolve any conflicts.

Blaming:

Blaming others is harmful. When we blame someone else for the problems in our life, we become a passive victim of circumstances and it becomes very difficult for us to change our situation. Many relationships are ruined by people who blame their partners when things go wrong. They take little responsibility for their problems. When something goes wrong at home or at work, they try to find someone to blame. They rarely admit their own problems, faults or mistakes.

Whenever we blame someone else for the problems in our life, we become helpless and powerless to change anything. The "blame game" hurts our personal sense of power. Don't assign blame. We have to take personal responsibility for our problems before we can hope to change them.

Acceptance:

We must stop trying to change others, as there is enough scope for change in ourselves. No one is perfect. Hence, there is a lot of room for improvement. Accept people as they are and not as you wish they were. Don't expect them to behave the way you want. As a matter of fact, the best thing is to not expect anything from anybody.

Reveal your feelings and thoughts:

Most people appreciate straightforward, honest communication. It shows you really care and want to work things out. Whenever you spot a problem area with someone, assume you each have different rules, and try to get clarity as to exactly what rules each of you have. The biggest problems tend to occur when people are simply unaware of each other's feelings and thoughts and they end up violating them without even realizing it. Reveal your feelings and guidelines to others and ask others about what they most need or want from you. You'll soon notice how much better your relationships are.

6

Relationships between couples

Love: relax, please

We always tend to show our affection easily when we fall in love with somebody. The process starts immediately. If love happens between two people, then we often do not even feel time. Love dwells within all of us. When you fall in love with somebody:

- You never lie to that person.

- You tend to back down with that person.

- You feel as though you have enormous power.

- We constantly think about that person.

Love has its own pain and every pain has its own pleasure.

That means we should not think that love is the only happiness. Lovers cannot be happy all the time; otherwise we will not get the real taste of love. Happiness can be followed by discord and vice versa.

We need to have a contrast. Only then can we see the real love and affection. For instance, you cannot see the stars in the day; each event has its counterpart, and through negative experiences we understand positive experiences; through mistakes, we grow. Have you ever imagined a life without death? Death forces a person to live in the present moment. We do not know whether the next day will arrive or not. If a person is willing to accept anything as it comes in life, then there is harmony for that person.

Love between two egocentric people is always in constant conflict. Neither one is ready to compromise nor they do not want to back down for any cause. When a person gets overly attached to freedom, they never compromise because of their freedom. More freedom implies more problems.

The most essential rule is to remember that love, alone, is not a relationship. Relating to each other is. There is no bottom line for relating because lovers may disappear but love always lives. There is no law in love, but present love is like an agreement. This agreement will not last forever without work. Love should be a commitment between two hearts, but it should not come from law or compulsion.

To understand the real feeling of love, lovers learn to relate to each other. One should not take a person for granted. Everyday changes happen for every person. We have got to understand that everything, every day, is new. Don't ever assume you know a person completely.

To achieve a long-lasting love, one has to explore the different possibilities of how to relate to one another. If you strive to know you partner more deeply, eventually you'll become mirrors for each other. Always try to find a way to relate to each other, because love is a constant adventure.

7

Love insights

A sculptor was hitting a stone and a traveler had asked him why he was doing it. The sculptor replied, "I see a beautiful statue inside this stone." In the same way, love is inside everybody, but sometimes is hidden beneath the "stone" we have constructed as a defense mechanism. The question is, how do we bring out the love within us? I had a chance to listen to Deepak Chopra's "Living without Limits." He mentioned a riveting point in his speech. "This universe runs on a coherence system with harmony. A 1 % change will affect 100% in the future." Essentially people should show their love and affection with full consciousness and without any expectation. That will affect a person later on. It is called the evolution of consciousness.

It is an obvious fact that we can learn and know what true love is. Does it even matter if we understand the many aspects of love? If we are in a happy relationship, we assume that everything is fine. Although your love with your partner might run smoothly for a while, it can take a turn we often may never have expected. This is why knowing about love approaches are helpful.

What may have turned you or your partner on at first, might not be a turn on later. How is this possible if you seemed so crazy over those things before? The reason is quite simple and reasonable. Novelty, or the "newness" of the relationship becomes commonplace. When we first get involved with people, the attraction is intense, but often based on surface information. As a relationship blooms, it becomes much more complex and requires more effort. The more you know about the person, the more you must come to accept.

We cannot blame a seed if it does not grow as we expected. The growth may be affected by many factors such as the soil, water or any kind of environmental problem. Do not form a conclusion immediately when you want to say adieu to your lover. Instead, analyze the relationship and give it some time before deciding. If your approach differs, do not look at it as something negative, but as an opportunity to combine them and form a creative love approach together. It should not be one way or the other. There is no such thing as the wrong way to love, except for obsession, control and abuse. The last three are not forms of love.

Considering and accepting our partner's different kind of love is extremely important. If you do not, it will seem like you are determined to have the romance in your relationship go your way—by your own approach. This will definitely cause unhappiness and quite possibly make your partner back away from a romance with you. Your partner will feel that there is a lack of attention towards his or her needs concerning romance. Remember to be considerate and learn to adapt to his or her ways too.

We should want to be with someone who intuitively understands our needs, who makes us want to feel like giving spontaneously, like being loving and thoughtful, simply because we feel grateful and even lucky to be with our partner. This exactly mirrors how we feel when we first fall in love. Our heart opens wide; being loving and thoughtful happens effortlessly. Later, we remember how we acted so lovingly when we felt such strong, intense feelings. We wonder why it is not the same now. We assume we're incompatible, or that this is just not the right person for us. The truth, however, is that when the infatuation ends, the real relationship begins. In the real relationship, true loving feelings are created by conscious loving acts. When both people experience true loving feelings on a consistent basis by consistently acting in a loving manner, there is no end to the spiral of love that can be created. So, choose now to give your relationship a gift that truly keeps on giving every day of the year.

- Support one another's goals and achievements.
- Respect each other.
- Take time to share dreams and goals on a regular basis with your partner.
- Consider daily dialogue as a means of improving your communication.
- Laugh together often.
- Fight fair. Be willing to forgive.
- Remember kindness towards one another is a great gift.
- Share your daily expectations.
- Make decisions about finances, disciplining the children, chores, vacations, etc., together.
- Take time to be alone together and work on your intimacy.
- Appreciate who your partner is and what they contribute to the world.
- Commit to staying together.
- Always find things you enjoy doing together.
- Be honest with one another.
- Try to see the positives in your mate.
- Always actively listen to each other.

8

Constant givers & constant receivers

It feels fabulous when our lover is being considerate of our approach, respects it, and follows it with us often. You cannot always be the one on the receiving end, however. You will then become a "constant receiver." "Constant receivers" are always on the lookout for their own interests. They never look beyond their own approach and the needs that are involved with it. They always observe whether or not they are getting what they need and want from their lovers, and if they feel they could be getting more, they grab more.

What about your partner?
What are his or her needs?
Have you even considered what their approach is and how you can compromise and follow it at times?
Have you tried to see things from their perspective?

Never let these questions go unanswered. If you find yourself being a "constant receiver," it does not mean you are a bad person. It only means that you have been a little selfish. When you realize this, stop yourself and look deep down. You will probably realize that you are aware of your over-receiving and have been so flattered by it that you got carried away. Once you have sorted this out, you can start returning the favor back to your partner.

On the flip side, being a "constant giver" also has its downside. You are always pleasing your partner, but what about you? Are you needs unimportant? Of course they are! Do not be too furious with your mate if this happens. Just remember what you just learned about "constant receivers." Your partner most likely did not ignore your needs on purpose, but just got carried away with being pampered. After all, you did create this situation. Many people fall under the category of giving too much. This is because most people believe it is more important to please their lovers than have their own needs and wants fulfilled. Caring about pleasing your partner is good, but disowning your own identity and needs is not. Get back on track by getting your guilt in order first. Know that you should not feel guilty for wanting or needing something from your partner. You are entitled to having those needs fulfilled. You also should not look at giving as the good thing and receiving as the bad thing. They are both good when equally exchanged. Start bringing your idealistic approaches and needs to your partner's attention. They, too, should give, instead of always receiving from you.

9

Love and meditation

In our lives, love is the closest phenomenon to meditation. What actually happens the moment you fall in love with someone? What transpires between those two who have fallen in love with each other? They drop their egos, at least for each other. They drop their hypocrisies and their masks. They want to be together—as though they are almost one soul within two bodies. Meditation is similar to this state the two share.

People who are not falling in love can never become meditators.

Love helps you to relax, which is part of meditation. Love helps you to be joyous, which is part of meditation. Love helps you, for a few moments at least, to be silent, which is the essential part of meditation. And finally, making love, if you reach an orgasmic experience, gives you a glimpse of what meditation is. Meditation is still a million times more powerful than this.

What is meditation?

Meditation is a technique available for gaining deep relaxation, eliminating stress, promoting health, increasing creativity and intelligence, and attaining inner happiness and fulfillment.

It is neither mind-control nor mental discipline. It is not concentration, Eastern philosophy, or a way of life. You don't have to control your breathing or muscles. You don't even have to try to relax. Meditation makes available to all of us a renewable energy source that we can tap into every day. Yet because most of us live in ignorance of it, we are forced needlessly to exhaust ourselves, and to stretch our physical and mental resources to a breaking point. All this while the energy, relaxation and inspiration we need is all around us.

Meditation enlivens the most profound level of the mind. It brings wide-ranging benefits to many areas of life. Which benefits do you need in your life?

Benefits of meditation:

- Unfolding the potential of the mind—personal effectiveness
- Reducing stress
- Improving health
- Reducing the negative effects of ageing
- Improving relationships
- Self Knowledge—fulfilling life's deepest need

Basic meditation is simply taking time for reflection and contemplation. You can learn more about meditation and meditation techniques by visiting: www.mou.org

PART II

PLANNING AND EXECUTION

10

Planning for a healthy relationship

To have a healthy relationship one should first understand the difference between a healthy and an unhealthy relationship.

In a healthy relationship you:

- Treat each other with respect.
- Feel secure and comfortable.
- Are not violent with each other.
- Can resolve conflicts satisfactorily.
- Enjoy the time you spend together.
- Support one another.
- Take interest in one another's lives: health, family, work, hobbies, etc.
- Have privacy and trust each other.
- Communicate clearly and openly.
- Have letters, phone calls, and e-mail that are your own.
- Encourage other friendships.
- Are honest about your past and present sexual activity if the relationship is intimate.

- Know that most people in your life are happy about the relationship.
- Have more good times in the relationship than bad.

In an unhealthy relationship, one or both of you:

- Tries to control or manipulate the other.
- Puts the other down.
- Dictates how the other dresses.
- Does not make time for the other.
- Criticizes the other's friends.
- Is afraid of the other's temper.
- Discourages the other from being close with anyone else.
- Ignores the other when one is speaking.
- Is overly possessive or gets jealous about ordinary behavior.
- Criticizes or supports others in criticizing people of the partner's gender, race, ethnicity, sexual orientation, religion, disability, etc.
- Controls the other's money or other resources.
- Harms or threatens to harm children, family members, pets, or objects of personal value.
- Uses physical force or threats to prevent the other from leaving
- Pushes, grabs, hit, punches, or throws objects.

Positive symbols in a relationship

There are plenty of people in this world who are emotionally and psychologically healthy and have some insight into themselves. The following is a list of the traits and behaviors that an ideal "healthy" dating partner will exhibit. While no one may fit all of these, use this as a general guide to assess the current "health" of your partner.

Healthy partners:

- Are comfortable in discussing their feelings about their past and present life experiences.
- Have good relationships with their family members, but are also living a physically and psychologically independent life.
- Respect your physical and emotional boundaries and reveal vulnerable information about themselves gradually over time.
- They are comfortable and secure enough within themselves to be satisfied with attention from you. They do not need to constantly seek out attention and admiration from others.
- They are psychologically finished with previous significant relationships.
- They have had enough time to get over the breakup of their previous major relationship.
- They are financially stable and seem to be able to handle financial issues without losing control.
- They can balance the need for control with the ability to be flexible when appropriate.
- They are able to express fears or vulnerability in emotionally safe situations.
- They are reliable, follow through on pre-arranged plans and show up on time for most meetings.
- They have one or more personal friendships that they have sustained for several years.

- They show an interest in you and your feelings and activities, as well as in their own.

- They have a lifestyle that is conducive to and allows for the addition of an intimate relationship. They are able to balance their work with their personal life and create enough time for both of them.

- They have a positive, optimistic outlook on life.

- They have a good sense of humor and presence of mind.

- They take responsibility for their life, their feelings and the consequences of their decisions without blaming others.

- They take care of themselves physically and emotionally. They dress in a clean, attractive manner, eat nutritiously, and exercise regularly.

- They are able to receive constructive feedback from others without getting defensive.

- They are ready to accept any criticism. They know very well that criticism comes through jealous people.

- They have many friends and acquaintances in their life and don't place expectations on them.

- They know how to resolve conflict in a constructive manner, or are willing to learn how to do so at any given time.

- They allow themselves to feel their anger and resentment and express anger in an appropriate or constructive manner.

Friends, these are the ideal qualities between two partners or friends, but in real life this list should act only as a guide. If you feel that some qualities are lacking in someone you really like, please try to explore and improve your relationship even more. On the other hand, if you find that your partner has less than 40 % of the qualities on this list, you may have to reevaluate or rethink whether or not the relationship is truly healthy for you.

11

How to live a pleased and fulfilled life

We often spend much of our time dealing with stress, worry and panic about what needs to be done for the future. We may be wired up over work and school along with everything else. The only way you can live a happy and satisfied life is when you start doing things that make you happy and satisfied. It can be easy if you just remember to make yourself one of your top priorities. Too many people neglect themselves and feel that it would be selfish if they took any time out to focus on their own being. While it is good to take care of others and other important things going on in your life, it is mandatory that you never forget about yourself. Discover who you really are and what matters most to you. Living a great life does not just happen. It requires planning and following that plan to a life that reflects who you truly are.

Most people avoid planning goals and dreams in their lives because they may have a fear of committing to them or failing in the endeavor. Sometimes we plan everything but are not able to persevere. We slow down, lose interest, and finally, achieve nothing. You may feel that making a mental note of your goals and dreams is enough, but you could very well be setting yourself up for disappointment and failure. By writing them down, you will have a visual reminder of your goals. Try writing them in a personal notebook that you can take a look at on a daily basis. Take some time every day to look over your goals and remind yourself of how important they really are to you.

You must know the reasons behind the importance of the dreams and goals you have. This way you can see more clearly why it is so necessary to follow through with your goals. Your excuses are demons. You must learn to fight them off if you wish to start living a happy and satisfied life. Making yourself one of your first priorities is not selfish. It is actually obligatory in order to succeed in the other aspects of your life. Without a happy and satisfied you, there will be no happy and satisfied life. You will be stressed out and unhappy. You might be consciously ignoring your needs and desires, but your subconscious mind has not forgotten about you. It will constantly remind you through stress, anger, sadness, insecurity and feelings of failure.

No one is going to work on your happiness for you, so you have to find the power and motivation within yourself. You must do meditation and use it to direct yourself into the path of true happiness and satisfaction. **Meditation is one of the main keys for keeping your goals alive and it charges you whenever you go downhill.** You can do anything you set your mind to and once you have stopped and gotten in touch with yourself, you will learn and realize just how wonderful and capable you really are. You will see that you have always been this capable. You will not only realize these things, but you will also begin to love who you are more and more. This will not only lead you to achieving the things that make you most happy, but will guide you into a world of many new dreams come true.

To achieve a long-lasting and happy relationship:

- You must feel good about yourself in order to sideline sad feelings. We seek love from the outside if we do not love ourselves.

- Dismantle your ego. This will help you gain more self-esteem.

- Develop self-confidence. This will make you avoid resentment and anger.

- Establish a mutual understanding or respect. A great relationship develops and depends on like-minded people. Show your human side.

- Allow people to offer themselves to you. Develop a common request. That will bond you forever.

- Use unconditional love.

- Praise people and make them comfortable before finding fault in them.

- Do not get agitated when you encounter a problem. Welcome the problem because we learn a lot through conflict.

- Ventilate or unload the thoughts that threaten your mind. Express these thoughts very openly.

- A successful relationship is above physical attraction and sex. Once a man or woman realizes the real deep inner love, they will not come out of that love. Physical activities will not help them satisfy it.

12

The concept of finding your soul mate

Soul mates are other souls that have agreed to connect with you on this planet for a purpose. In some cases it is to clear up karma. In other cases it is to complete unfinished business, and for some it is to accomplish a particular goal together. These relationships may be a joy to be in or these relationships may be a pain in your life. Either way they are here for a reason.

Spiritual Soul Mates:

Many religions and spiritual paths believe in reincarnation and the concept of karma. Through reincarnation, soul mates may have spent many lifetimes together in past lives. Other spiritual methods of searching for one's soul mate are astrology, numerology, palm reading, personality types, and magic. Modern spiritual paths often blend western and eastern philosophies.

Companion Soul Mates:

These are people that we encounter throughout life. These are usually friends, teachers, mentors, or other people who have helped you achieve a life's goal or helped you during times of crisis.

Twin Soul Mates:

Sometimes you may think that you knew each other before. That is called twin souls. We believe that two people who knew each other in a former life are almost mirror images of each other in this life. We feel a bond, affection, attraction, and similarity and it almost as if you know each other previously. It is a beautiful feeling. Wherever we are, we feel comfortable while thinking about them. The beauty is the connection between the loved ones. We are emotionally bonded with them.

These types of soul mates are your closest friends or a person with whom you really click. According to those who believe in reincarnation, you have already met them in a past life. In this life you are continuing the relationship. There is an emotional bond between these soul mates and each is able to sense the feelings of the other.

This is the most popular type of soul mate. There is usually one twin flame soul mate for each of us. Twin flame soul mates have spent multiple lifetimes together in past lives. There is incredible chemistry and attraction towards each other. They "complete" each other and only few lucky people are able to find their twin flame soul mate. Twin flame soul mates, if separated, usually suffer enormous pain.

When soul mates first meet they sometimes feel as if they already know each other. They may feel very familiar to each other. Soul mates can have a beautiful relationship together, but it will take work. Soul mate relationships may last a lifetime and others may only be for a particular purpose and be temporary. You can have more than one Soul Mate in a lifetime.

We have at least six soul mates with our surroundings, they are your father, mother, brother, sister, relative, friend, lover, spiritual boss, and life partner. We have been learning lessons of love, affection, knowledge, and support (moral as well as financial).

Sometimes we like somebody initially, but after some time we come to know that he or she is not the right person us. Once you have realized that these dates will not lead to the relationship you have dreamed of, then obviously the person is not your dream mate either, and it would be best if you stop seeing each other to prevent any misleading expectations. Continuing to date someone just because you have entered a comfort zone, or do not want to hurt his or her feelings, will only hold you back from meeting who you are truly meant to be with. Also, it will waste precious time for both you and your date. Gently break it to him or her that you find them to be a very interesting and nice person, but you feel like you need to go solo for a while. Then move on.

13

Discovering your soul mate

Before finding your soul mate, you must first understand your own requirements such as mental or physical preferences, emotional characteristics, and other ingredients of your basic nature. Sit in a calm place or somewhere you like, and search yourself deeply until you understand the real attributes or qualities you possess.

Here are the right signs for your soul mate:

1. We often feel that even though we have just met it is as though we already know that person.

2. We feel that we have known each other for years.

3. When you are with that person you feel like a complete person.

4. You are strongly attracted to each other physically.

5. You are strongly attracted to each other's personalities.

6. Our mind threatens that you cannot live without him or her.

7. You have common interests.

8. You want to share values and problems.

9. You respect each other and are willing to sacrifice your feelings for them especially when they hurt.

10. They are someone who makes you feel truly special, precious, and worthy.

11. They put great effort into showing you their enthusiasm for you and the things you find important.

12. You meet on the same emotional levels or same frequency match.

13. You tend to back down even though we do not like something the other does.

14

Cultivating the long-lasting relationship

Unconditional love, friendship, and intimacy will cultivate a healthy relationship. Explore the various possibilities for relating to each other with mutual concern, joint growth opportunity, open communication, support, and living in the moment, full of interest.

When we make a commitment to a relationship, we have some degree of unconditional regard for the relationship. The relationship is reciprocal and we are present when it is easy and meets our needs, as well as when it is a difficult struggle and we feel like we are doing all the giving. To make such a commitment, we must be capable of selfless service beyond the needs of our ego and the relationship must have a deeper vision or meaning, which transcends those unpleasant times.

All healthy relationships require consistent, ongoing, and conscious attention to survive and thrive. It is a simple fact that whenever we put our attention on something, we are choosing to create more of it. Similarly, whatever we ignore, we are choosing to let go of and allow to fade out of our lives. We have to make what we desire in our lives. We live in a world with more distractions to steal our attention than humanity has ever experienced at any time before.

We can consciously attend to other people, but if we do so from an attitude of manipulation and control, the outcome will be a one-sided unhealthy relationship. An attitude of respect, on the other hand, nourishes the heart of both participants and assures that each person's needs are attended to. Related to respect is gratitude. When we commit to a relationship, give it conscious attention, and feel respect for the person or entity we are in relationship with, we naturally are grateful for their presence in our lives. We honor the gifts they bring us and communicate our gratitude on a regular basis in whatever form feels right.

We must be able to trust when things appear to be going nowhere in our lives. We must have faith that there is something going on that we cannot comprehend or see. Similarly, when we are quiet and mindful and listen to ourselves, we must trust the impulses from that small, still voice within when it suddenly urges us to go off in a new direction.

Reflect upon how much conscious attention you give to yourself and others. See if you are relating to them with respect and gratitude. Notice if you have a basic sense of trust with yourself and others. Be aware of how much genuine bonding you do with the important people in your life and with yourself. Consciously reflecting on these questions can open the door to richer, deeper, healthier and more alive relationships on all levels of your life.

Commitment to the truth can be uncomfortable and scary at times, but it is also the surest path to ongoing growth and deepening connection available to conscious relationship partners. Encourage everyone to make that commitment and pass it on through words and deeds to others, as well as our children. If you have struggled with this in the past, be honest about that. Take steps to understand why you might have been less than honest before. What healing needs to take place within you so that you no longer need to hide or appear different than who you really are? And remember, the commitment to the truth is not a commitment to always talking about something negative! The truth can be how grateful you feel to be in this relationship or how wonderful it feels to be with someone who shares your vision of an intimate relationship.

We are all capable of greater acts of love and truth than we may believe. We are all capable of being clearer, more honest, loving, and less selfish. By honoring the original vision that called us to love at this time, we can commit to the truth of what we are experiencing and to communicating it to our partners on a regular basis. This process will truly set you and your partner free to experience the deepest and highest connection possible.

Patience is key to a healthy relationship. There are times when your partner may not respond in a way in which is pleasing to you, but this does not mean you have to take it so seriously or personally. Slow down, take a deep breath and think of reasons why your partner may be acting a certain way. Assuming and jumping to conclusions is always an unhealthy step to take because it shows your partner that they are not entitled to act freely and which can cause them to feel attacked. It also shows that you automatically assume the worst about them. Give your partner some time and let them know that you will be there for him or her when he or she is ready to talk. No matter what the situation may be, patience is golden in a relationship, unless your partner never wants to discuss matters with you. This is unhealthy.

Honesty is something absolutely imperative in a harmonious relationship. A person needs to know that he or she can trust his or her partner because it builds a zone of safety and comfort. They need to know that they can at least rely on their loving partner to tell them the truth, no matter what. Being human means being imperfect. We will make mistakes. However, we should not let that fact lead us to make mistakes we already know are wrong ahead of time.

If either you or your partner deliberately makes mistakes, it shows a lacks respect and consideration for the other. This is unhealthy for the relationship. What is healthy, however, is realizing the mistake you committed *is* a mistake. You or your partner needs to know what was done wrong and need to take responsibility for what was done. Once you or your partner has realized this, you can then figure out how to confess your wrongdoings to the other.

We cannot change our partner's character, but we *can* change the present and future quality of our relationship.

15

Target setting in your relationship

When you think about it, relationships are all about goal setting. Once you fall in love, you both start focusing on the goals you each have for the relationship; this includes where you want it to lead and what your relationships beliefs are. One of the main reasons many couples break up is because they never shared their relationship goals with each other. Most people just let the relationship do its own work and flow naturally; while that is okay in some cases, it is important to keep in touch with one another's goals for the relationship.

Besides the fact that you are attracted to each other, share common interests and have fallen in love, what are your goals for the relationship? Though you can never predict what will really happen in the future of the relationship, you do already have an idea of what you wish to give and receive from this romantic partnership. It is important that you fully understand what your goals are first, before having this talk with your partner. Are you looking for a serious partner or just someone you can spend time with so that you are not lonely? Would you like the relationship to eventually lead to marriage, or is marriage not the most important goal for you at this time? When you figure out exactly what your goals are in the relationship, you will then need to learn why those goals are so important for you right now. For example, if marriage is a goal for you, why is getting married so important to you at this point in your life? You need to understand your reasons for your goals and make sure you are setting those goals for the right reasons.

Once you have figured out your goals, you should then share them with your partner. Likewise, be able to listen to what his or her goals are. You both need to see exactly where you both stand individually and as a couple. If there are similarities, you both need to find ways of achieving these goals. If there are differences in the goals you both have, you then need to find a compromise you both feel is fair to the relationship. Not having the same exact relationship goals does not mean that you are not meant to be together, but it does mean that more communication is necessary. You can always keep track of where your relationship is leading and where it is lacking anything that it needs. Plan ways on you can both accomplish each of your relationship goals, and talk about which methods you both feel will work best. Goals can change over time too, which is exactly why you and your partner should touch base on each of your thoughts, so you never reach a point where the relationship feels lost and confusing for one or both of you.

Though it is important to understand your partner's goals, it is just as important to keep in touch with what you really want and need from the relationship. Losing your direction can cause you to stay in a relationship even if it no longer fulfills your needs and desires. Partners can change and there is nothing you can do to change them unless they choose to change. The power you do have is in holding on to the dreams you have for yourself. Neither of you should have to lower your expectations for the other just because you want to stay with your partner. You should always work together in keeping the relationship on track. With direct communication and constructive and attainable goal setting, your relationship can grow stronger and more fulfilling.

16

Gratitude and forgiveness will enhance any relationship

Most spiritual and psychological traditions speak of the importance of cultivating a sense of gratitude in order to evolve into higher realms of human existence and consistently experience joy, vitality and meaning in one's life. This is especially true in the western world, where we are bombarded with the lure and illusory promise of material things from the moment we are born.

Gratitude

Where does gratitude come in? We need a major attitude shift if we are to create healthier relationships, more inner serenity, fulfillment and meaningful lives. Cicero once wrote, **"Gratitude is not only the greatest of virtues, but the parent of all the others."** Gratitude paves the way for a host of other very positive qualities to emerge.

How we can cultivate a greater sense of gratitude within others and ourselves? We can begin by starting a gratitude journal where we write down all things, both great and small, that we are grateful for in our life. Nothing is too small or insignificant to be included, because the scale of gratitude knows no bounds. You can be as grateful for the flower that bloomed today as for the home you live in, the health of your family and the look in your dog's eye when you come home. Review your list daily.

In terms of our relationships, we tend to take our spouses, lovers, significant others and friends for granted. There is no greater gift than to tell a loved one how much you appreciate their presence in your life. Countless times while working with couples, I have seen resentment and anger melt away in the presence of sincere gratitude and appreciation. Call a friend or relative or write a letter to let that person know what they mean to you, even if they are healthy and not in crisis. It's also a wonderful practice to have an entire family express gratitude together on a regular basis. The earlier children start, the greater their capacity for gratitude becomes.

The consistent practice of expressing gratitude also reminds us that we do not live alone. We survive only because we are constantly receiving gifts of all kinds from people, nature and spirit. Gratitude helps us to be more aware of the many things that we receive from other people; it helps us realize that our lives depend on the perpetual giving of others. It allows us to feel a deeper responsibility to give more of ourselves. Albert Einstein said, **"A hundred times every day I remind myself that my inner and outer life depends on the labors of other men, living and dead, and that I must exert myself in order to give in the measure as I have received and am still receiving."**

To speak gratitude is to be courteous and pleasant. To enact gratitude is generous and noble, but to live gratitude is to touch heaven. When an encounter triggers a warm, comfortable feeling, this is reflecting something you like about yourself. The appropriate and very important expression is gratitude. Every positive encounter reflects the beauty within you waiting to be expressed; gratitude is the releasing mechanism. Gratitude is essential to reinforce your awareness of your reality in love.

Gratitude will enhance you life in the following ways:

- Gratitude unlocks the fullness of life.

- It teaches us to be content with what we have, which increases the value of people and things we may take for granted. It turns denial into acceptance, chaos to order and confusion to clarity. It can turn a meal into a feast, a house into a home and a stranger into a friend.

- Gratitude makes sense of our past, brings peace for today and creates a vision for tomorrow.

Appreciation will strengthen the relationship:

The sweet words of appreciation whispered in the ear during distant days of courtship might have long since dried up like flower petals and blown away in the winds of daily survival. Apparently the telepathic waves of "just knowing" don't carry criticisms quite so well, as people are often willing enough to express criticisms by way of words. What is the net result? Criticisms may outweigh appreciations ten to one, and discontent reigns.

It's easy enough to assume that one's caring acts, whether they be cooking good meals, cleaning the car, building a shelf, contributing a hard-earned paycheck to the common cause, etc., constitute ample statements of appreciation of your partner. While these acts are essential, consider for a moment whether they really articulate your sincere love at just the right moment.

If you have a piece of property that "appreciates" in value, the value increases exponentially. Likewise, if you show appreciation to a person who has been trying hard and is feeling worn down, that person, just like the property value, grows. His or her spirit swells. The energy goes up and the willingness to give increases. Good feelings and the capacity for relating grow.

Appreciating your self inwardly is also vitally important and it helps to counteract a tendency to rely on your partner for self-esteem. Appreciation can be magical. It is food for the soul. It helps people feel connected, known and loved. Appreciation does not have to be grand to be valuable. While "I think you're fantastic!" may strum the harp of one person's soul, something simple like "You have a delightful sense of color in the way you dress," or "I love your smile," may be sweet water for another person's wilted garden.

Accompanying the appreciation with a "thank you" extends its power. "Even though I really wish you were around more, I appreciate the incredible amount of hard work and tenacity you've put into creating your business. Thanks for really caring about us all surviving well!" The overworked partner, now feeling appreciated, may be able to relax defended postures of superiority, defiance or non-cooperation. He or she may suddenly feel inclined to consider ways to stay home a bit more and spend some quality time with family. A greater willingness to join and problem-solve has been generated.

The most challenging time to show appreciation is when you are in the midst of a disagreement or an argument. Try to pause, actively listen to what your partner is saying. Then, if possible, verbally appreciate whatever good intention you perceive may underlie your partner's point of view, even if you disagree heartily with the opinion or way it is being put forward.

If you and your partner are rusty with appreciations, giving them will undoubtedly feel a bit awkward at first. But as long as they are sincere, you may be delighted by a new level of good will that begins to spring up in your relationship like fresh green grass. If you've been feeling down about your partner, it may be helpful to start out with little things that you may have been taking for granted for too long, like the well-made bed, maintained car, kindness to neighbors and friends, gentleness with children and playful jokes.

There may be no quicker way to initiate welcome relief from the painful squeaking of a relationship wheel than the exchange of good, solid and real appreciation. Above all, identifying and sharing what you love, honor and respect about each other may help you and your partner reclaim some of those wonderful reasons you fell in love in the first place!

Forgiveness

When an encounter triggers fear in some form (anger, guilt, frustration, disappointment, annoyance) this is reflecting something you don't like about yourself. Now the appropriate and very important expression is forgiveness. Forgiveness can be one of the most difficult and complicated aspects of life. It is not that we don't love compassionate people who desire to be thoughtful and forgiving. It is simply that the concept of forgiveness has been so reshaped and redefined that to truly establish a comfortable and clear conception of its substance and purpose can be challenging. We need to *feel*, in the deepest area of our spirit, the essence of forgiveness and to allow for the metamorphosis of that energy to occur. We must let go of any pre-conceived idea, perception, learned definition or past experience having to do with what forgiveness is or feels like. For now, let us replace this previous notion of *forgiveness* with a clean slate so that we may begin with a clear, fresh foundation on which to work.

Forgiveness does not mean forgetting something has happened, but allows your voice within to guide you to a different way of seeing what happened. This helps free you from your grievance.

Forgiveness will enhance you life in the following ways:

- It will penetrate your experience and engulf it with love.

- Free your heart of hurt from the memory.

- Allow you to move on.

- Give the opportunity to receive the gifts from the experience.

- Allow the lessons to be learned and provide you with the chance to accept what is true.

- Deepen your strength of character and clarify your sense of self.

- Relieve you of the burden of anger and guilt.

- Give you back your power.

- Rather than have the experience direct you, you can own, give value to and positively utilize the experience in your life.

While most will acknowledge that forgiveness is a wonderful concept, very few people know how to practice it effectively. Understand that forgiving does not mean forgetting or giving permission for the behavior to be repeated. It does not mean that what was done was acceptable. Forgiveness is often needed for behaviors that were not acceptable and that you should not allow to be repeated.

Recognize that you are the only one who is being hurt by your non-forgiveness. You feel the anger—the tightness in your stomach. You are the one rehearsing in your mind what you would like to say or do to "punish" them. When there is no forgiveness, the bitterness lingers; when you could be enjoying today's pleasures, you are upsetting yourself with yesterday's injustices. You give control of your emotions to the person who hurt you. It's been said that the best revenge is your own calmness. If you look inside and realize that you are harboring one or more resentments that cause bitterness in your heart and would like to initiate a process of forgiveness, here are some tips on how to proceed. You may have to repeat this process several times if it turns out you were not ready to fully release your hurt, and if you are still too consumed by anger.

- Make a list of what specific actions you need to forgive. What was actually done that caused your pain?

- Acknowledge your part in each of the items on your list. Did you stay when you could or should have left? Did you draw this energy to you in some manner? If so, then you, too, have some responsibility.

- Realize that the other person did the best that he or she could have done at the time. Why did the person hurt us? They, like you, are an imperfect human being. Instead of thinking that you would never commit such an offense, realize that if you had been that person, you could have done exactly the same thing. The incident was not about you. It was about the wrongdoer's misguided attempt to meet his or her own needs.

- Realize the futility of grudges. Sometimes we hold a grudge as if that would punish the person, but it rarely has that effect, nor does it assure that he or she will behave considerately in the future. Many persons actually prefer holding on to resentments because of the hidden "fringe benefits" or payoffs. Examine what your possible pay-offs may be in playing the victim or martyr roles.

- Acknowledge to yourself, in writing or out-loud, what you have gained from the relationship with the person who hurt you.

- Center yourself and verbally forgive yourself first for anything you may have done, on any level, to contribute to this hurt and resentment.

- In a similar manner, express forgiveness for the hurts on your list, one by one. Allow yourself to experience the full range of feelings that emerge.

- It may also be helpful to create a ceremony in which you get rid of your resentments, symbolizing the ending of the link between you. You may choose to visualize placing them on a raft and watching it drift gently away down a river. You may prefer to burn them and scatter the ashes of your resentment list.

- Visualize the person you are forgiving being blessed by your forgiveness and, as a result, free them from continuing the behavior that hurt you.

Right now as you think of a hurt or resentment inside, remember that you have a choice. You can decide to be responsible for what you are feeling. Use these guidelines to resolve and release the bitterness, hurt and resentment that is clogging up your heart and life, so that the life and love can again flow through you. In turn, it will flow to others you come in contact with. It also opens up the possibility of greater love and intimacy for you as well.

17

Building the bond in your relationship

A bond is when two people are connected. You are attracted to each other. Common values and interests brought the two of you together as a couple, but the bond has not been set completely. Besides the fact that you have love and care between you, you also need to see whether or not the two of you are friends. Is it possible to be friends? It is a must if the two of you are going to build a lasting bond.

Having a strong longing and passion for another is important, but is not enough fuel to keep the bond going. With friendship, your relationship will have strength to withstand all kinds of circumstances. There will be times, for example, when you as a couple are not living in your most passionate times. This is natural and does not mean there is no longer love or desire. As your relationship deepens, you will go through many experiences and stages that may put your romance aside for a while. This is where friendship comes in and why it is so important. You should be there for each other and understand your partner's situations and concerns. Just take a look at your friends. See what makes your friendship with them so great. You then need to see if your partner has those same similarities or exact qualities. Another point to think of is to keep yourself aware of what behavior you would not accept from a friend. You should definitely not accept those behaviors from your partner either.

It is not easy to put our friends and lovers in the same comparison, because we are in love with our partners, and therefore will be more patient with them than we would with our friends. You can easily blind yourself due to the love you feel for that person and not even realize when he or she is not being a good friend and partner to you. How can you tell? A true friendship is basically the same as the true qualities that define real love. The difference is we are in love and have a deep desire for our partners. We share a commitment and a goal of building a future. Perhaps we even plan on getting married and having a family together. The list below will help you see if your lover is a friend to you as well.

1. You can talk to and confide in each other about anything.

2. Your partner is there for you when you need to talk to someone.

3. Both can rely on each other when needed.

4. You have a permanent shoulder to cry on when needed.

5. You have many things in common.

6. You accept one another for who you are.

7. You listen to one another and consider each other's opinions important.

Do not feel guilty for having higher expectations from your lover either. People often feel like they should be more lenient and understanding when it comes to their lovers. Even though it is important to keep an understanding attitude to avoid misunderstandings and arguments, you should never let things always slide or make excuses for your partner's wrong doings. You should expect better and not accept such behavior. You deserve better. After all, you invest most of your emotions and time into your partner, so always remember that you are entitled to receive the same in return.

As important as having that great friendship is, it is also good to remember not to let the friendship get out of hand. It is wonderful when you can be best friends with your partner, but sometimes the friendship is doing so well that it receives all the focus. In the meantime love gets neglected. If you are not careful, in time, you will start looking at each other as close buddies and no longer be that passionate couple you started as. There are points that can guide you into detecting when your romance and desire is entering the danger zone before it is too late. You want to stop it before you need to seek professional advice on how to get things back on track.

Remembering not to forget our desires for our partner will keep romance in the picture. If the relationship still fails to renew those feelings and you or your partner cannot leave that buddy mode, and is looking around with curiosity for others, then your relationship will need some extra help.

As long as you and your partner remember to keep love and friendship balanced, your relationship will continue to live in great health for as long as you both desire. Relationships can seem confusing and hopeless at times, and they can get that way if you do not keep close watch. Stop yourself periodically to check the status of your relationship. Make sure the bond is building as it should be. The two of you can build the greatest bond. Most importantly, remember that key word here is balance.

The highest level of love is trust. If you believe in love and in your lover, then that will cause you to do anything for your lover. The difference between love and regard is very simple:

Love: Love is accepting. If you are in-love with someone who initially told you he doesn't drink alcohol and you find out later it is a lie, love might make you ignore his indiscretion and encourage him to keep drinking.

Regard: Regard is selective. If you have high regard for someone and the same situation occurs, you will lose interest in him once you find out that he has lied and mislead you.

Trust, trust, and only trust will bring a person into your love universe. For that you need patience, sacrifice, and determination. Ego will not allow a love to grow, instead that will always make a person think superficially. It will bring you down in your life. If anybody wants to lose their ego, they have to learn meditation.

PART III

MANAGING AND RESCUING YOUR RELATIONSHIP

18

Why do we hurt the ones we love?

One of the most common problems in relationships is that we feel emotionally wounded by each other on a regular basis. You both love each other and want to stay together, yet you keep hurting each other through verbal abuse, physical rejection, taking each other for granted, betraying emotional trust, or by bringing up vulnerable topics from a partner's past.

Why do we do behave like this?

We all experience various degrees of emotional hurt and trauma while growing up. Unfortunately, we have formed obsessions around whatever we experienced. We may feel revitalized living the same way we did as children and so we may do things unconsciously to get our partner to trigger those feelings. For example, a person who grew up with a lot of distance may feel uncomfortable with closeness and may damage it by picking fights or avoiding intimacy. A person who grew up in a disorganized, dramatic home may be uncomfortable with harmony and quiet and always seem to trigger confusion or drama in their relationships.

We all tend to try to find the love we never experienced as children. If we did not or cannot get that love from our original parent or caretaker, the next best thing is to get the love from someone who has a very similar personality to the person who originally wounded us. We generally feel a lot of attraction, chemistry and intensity in our love with such partners due to the interconnected nature of our emotional thoughts.

What we may not realize, though, is that once we get into a deeper, committed relationship, our fear often gets activated. When we become afraid, we will strike out in exactly the same way that our parents or caretakers did. Eventually we get wounded again. The amount of pain becomes worse after getting into a deeper, committed relationship because the very person we hoped could give us the love we never received, is now hurting us.

Sometimes we may lack the knowledge and skills of how to communicate our feelings constructively. Timing is very important. Many people often hurt their partners or loved ones and they want to change that behavior. However, they do not use the proper way to communicate what they are feeling in a constructive manner. Our culture does very little to teach us how to relate to our own feelings and how to express or communicate those feelings to others in a safe manner.

19

How do we stop hurting the ones we love?

- Think twice before conveying your feelings to your partner, and make sure that whatever you say is appropriate and pertinent to your problem with your partner.

- Take some time for yourself before showing any of your negative feelings.

- We need to learn how to make it safe for our partners to express how they feel.

- Create a loving presence where you authentically listen and validate your partner's experience.

- Try expressing your feelings in ways that bring you closer to intimacy.

- Whenever you feel resentful, take some time for yourself. This will avoid an immediate collision.

- Talk to your partner in an open manner. Understand how and why you trigger each other to lash out in hurtful and destructive ways.

Please respect the fact that in an intimate and committed relationship, you must take out the ego completely. We are all on a journey of awakening and intimate relationships, which provide us a powerful opportunity to see ourselves and our psychological and spiritual lessons more clearly. We can hide ourselves from people in general, but we cannot hide from the person we love and who loves us. True love never hides. Understand the difference between sympathy and love. Enjoy the love and its pain. It is a wonderful experience that will teach a lot of lessons.

All that matters will eventually come to light through this unexplained and wonderful process we call "love.' When it does, we can choose to defend, judge, attack or run away. Or we can choose to be present, to look inside with acceptance and love for ourselves, and to feel gratitude that this aspect of ourselves has revealed itself. Then we can clearly see that any part of ourselves that hurts others is simply a part of ourselves that needs more love. From this perspective we hurt the one we love so that we can learn to love others and ourselves unconditionally, more deeply, and more completely. And by loving and healing ourselves, we ultimately heal our partner's wounds as well. In this way we make it safer for them to fully be who they are and to experience the deeper oneness and magic that only love can bring to our lives.

20

Warning signs of relationship breakdown

One of the most useful recent research findings is the work that has identified the early warning signs of a weakening intimate relationship. This information is crucial in accepting when your relationship is in serious need of more attention or help.

Relationship Breakdown Checklist

To evaluate the current health of your relationship, ask yourself the following questions:

- Does he/she insist on having control over your life, thoughts, and behavior?

- Does he/she intimidate you by screaming or by threatening to withdraw his/her relationship or to leave you if you do not do as he/she wishes?

- Does he/she switch from charm to anger without warning?

- Does he/she project the blame for all his/her failures and short-comings onto you?

- Is he/she extremely jealous and possessive?

- Does he/she force you to participate in sexual acts that are unpleasant to you?

- Does he/she disgrace you in front of others?

- Is he/she charming in public, but a different person in private?

- Is he/she in competition with important people in your life for attention?

- Does he/she isolate you from your family and friends?

- Does he/she break your possessions or objects, or his/her possessions or objects?

- Is he/she hypersensitive and easily upset by annoyances that are part of daily life?

- Does he/she have a past history of abuse?

- Does he/she emotionally abuse you? (Ex. insults, belittling comments, ignoring you, acting sulky or angry when you initiate an action or idea)

- Does he/she drink heavily, use drugs, or try to get you drunk?

- Does he/she go through extreme highs and lows—kind one minute and cruel the next?

- Does he/she suddenly change to words like "me" instead of "we?"

- Instead of merely complaining, does he/she attack and blame your personality and/or character by saying things such as: "you are a selfish, uncaring person."

- Is he/she physically violent to you or others, even if it's "just" grabbing and pushing to get his/her way?

- Is he/she angry and threatening to the extent that you have changed your life so as not to anger him/her?

- Is he/she possessive or does he/she act like you're a piece of property?

- Has he/she stopped returning your phone calls?

- Does he/she have endless excuses for why you can't get together?

- Does he/she display affection less frequently? (Ex. not holding you, not returning a hand squeeze)

If you discover that you have checked several of these items, it is time to reevaluate the relationship.

21

How to restore the broken belief

Trust is the foundation of any relationship. Whether it is a business or intimate relationship, without trust the whole structure of a personal connection simply falls apart. Even if you communicate with great skill, but trust has been broken, you won't get anywhere. The person you're speaking with will simply see your attempts as insincere and they won't hear anything you say until trust has been repaired. Often I see couples that have been hurt so many times by each other that all trust has been destroyed. Additional skills are needed in order to repair trust once it has been broken.

Before discussing how to repair trust, it's useful to understand how it gets broken in the first place. There are two primary ways to damage or destroy the trust in a relationship. First, you can break an agreement with a person. If the agreement is important enough, it may take only one broken promise to destroy the trust you've built together. For example, when one partner has an affair, it can shatter a relationship. The second way to damage trust is through hurting a person in various ways. As with broken promises, sometimes a single hurt can destroy trust. Whatever way trust has been broken, there is a specific process you can go through in order to repair the damage.

Think back to a time when someone broke an agreement with you and you both knew it wasn't your fault. What did you want from that person? If you are like most people, you didn't want to hear that person's excuses and rationalizations. As the excuses babbled on, you probably became even more upset. Instead of giving you excuses, you probably wanted the person to acknowledge how hurt or angry you felt and to take responsibility for being at fault. If a person is upset, it's a good idea to acknowledge his or her pain, even if you don't know the cause of the bad feelings. Avoid defending yourself, trying to fix situation immediately, or turning away. Simply allow this person to feel his or her feelings. Such actions can go a long way in healing the hurt.

To acknowledge people's hurt or angry feelings, you can ask why they feel bad and then compassionately listen. Since they are upset, they are likely to declare their feelings in an angry manner. Instead of defending yourself, your job is to see if you can gain a better understanding of what's going on. If there is anything about the story you don't understand, ask people to explain their feelings fully without any hesitation. The more you understand what is going on, the easier it will be to mend the broken trust.

If, after listening to someone, you still don't understand why he/she got so upset, you need to further explore the reasoning and feelings that have been discussed. If you have not done something obviously wrong and yet a person is quite upset, he or she must have interpreted some behavior or event differently than you. I have found the question, "Why do you think I did that?" to be profoundly useful in clearing up misunderstandings and hurts.

We naturally assume people react to words and behaviors the same way we do, but that is always not the case. Only when we know what's really going on in a person's head can we repair the hurts that mound up from misunderstandings. The more information we have and the more accurate it is, the easier it is to repair the damage.

Once you know why someone is hurt, start talking slowly in an appropriate environment and express your feelings naturally in a different way. It is especially useful to say your positive reason or motivation for your actions, such as "I was trying to avoid that situation" or "save you from being hurt," or "I was trying to avoid a problem." By clarifying your intention, the hurt can often be repaired before it goes into broken trust. If a person's upset is not due to a misunderstanding, but rather due to a broken agreement, you need to take responsibility for what you did and apologize. This is not an easy thing to do, but because it is so rare, a sincere apology can go a long way towards repairing broken trust.

Once misunderstandings have been cleared up, or appropriate apologies have been given, the last step is to let the person you've hurt know how much you care. When people feel hurt, what hurts is the thought they are being rejected in some way. The obvious antidote to the hurt is telling someone why the relationship is so important to you. As soon as someone is convinced that you really care, trust will be restored.

For little misunderstandings or small errors, it doesn't take long to repair broken trust. Yet, if problems have gone unrepaired for a long time, it can be quite a task to convince someone that you really care. That's why it's always best to heal broken trust as soon as it has been broken.

When a partner has been very badly hurt, he or she will usually need to fully express the hurt and anger before really forgiving you. This is often best done within the context of individual therapy. If the hurt partner tries to directly express her anger and hurt to her mate, it will frequently just turn into an argument. Yet, in individual therapy, you can get all those bad feelings out without doing additional harm.

Trust, like love, can't be smelled, touched, or tasted, and yet it has massive power. Although it is invisible to our eyes, it is evident in our hearts. You can't have successful relationships without trust. It is important to make consistent efforts to keep the trust between you and others growing strong. The moment you notice trust has been damaged in a relationship, work to repair it as soon as possible. Like a recent wound, broken trust can get infected and spread if the right aid is not quickly applied. Yet, just as bones can grow stronger as they heal from being broken, so can trust grow stronger from being properly repaired.

22

How to cope with a broken heart

Being heartbroken is a pain that people are unable to truly understand until they have experienced it for themselves. If you have, you are aware of how fragile your heart was at the time. Healing a broken heart will take time, but it is not impossible even though it may feel that way at the time. It is never an easy process to go through, but with the right prescription, you will be on your way to recovery and happiness again. The following tips can help ease the turmoil of a break-up:

- Please do not make rash decisions when your heart is broken because time is the best healer.

- A change of place will heal your mind. Try to relocate for a while and talk to different people.

- Discontinuing a serious relationship is emotionally challenging and can drive you to do things that are unhealthy for your self-being, such as using drugs, alcohol, promiscuous sex, etc. To avoid entering such hazardous areas, keep yourself occupied.

- Meditation has the capacity to help us cope with the situation.

- I always ask people to cry. Crying makes things clearer. Cry alone or cry with someone whom you feel comfortable with. At the same time, remember that nothing other than emotional release comes from crying. Releasing and dwelling are two different things.

- After doing a detailed analysis of all possibilities, if you feel that you are right then realize that he or she has lost a good partner or friend in you. They will realize the mistake soon.

- It is best to spend as little time alone as you can in the first few weeks of your breakup. This will help your emotions slowly and patiently return to their normal pattern.

- Look at the relationship as a learning experience and an opportunity to improve your relationship skills. It is a way to realize what you truly need and want from a romantic relationship.

- Human psychology says that the human mind changes at least once in a six-month period because of external influence.

- Hating your partner will only build up tension and stress in your life, which prevents your emotions from getting back to order.

- Appreciate their honesty of no longer wanting to pursue the relationship, instead of giving you high hopes for a possible future together. It is always better to leave a relationship that didn't have a chance than to be misled.

- Learn to forgive yourself and that will speed up the healing process. You will feel more peaceful and calm about the situation.

- Teach yourself that there is more to life than romantic relationships by spending quality time with your friends and family.

- Learning to be your own best friend will not only improve your relationship with yourself, but with others as well. As you begin to discover the other beauties of life and yourself, you will become more stable and gain the strength to face anything that crosses your path. Meditate.

- Conquer your fear of being alone. You need to help yourself understand that it is not abnormal to be on your own and that your values come from whom you are rather than whom you are with.

- Remember that when a relationship ends it means that the two of you were no longer compatible and that always takes two, not just you.

Essentially you should keep in mind is that it is acceptable to feel sad about what happened. It is perfectly normal to feel sad and cry after a break-up. You have invested most of your time and all of your love and interest into your ex-partner; therefore you will go through a sad and painful withdrawal. It is notable that you not grieve all on your own. There will definitely be times when you will just want to be alone and undisturbed. However, it is important that you talk to your friends and family about it. Talking about it is not only healthy, but will mend your heart quicker because you will release the thoughts and facts that are hurting you so much. Talk to a person whom you feel has good suggestion; it will help you to gather your strength, pick yourself up, and console yourself.

Before you consider entering another relationship, take a step back and ask yourself why you want to do so. Make sure that you are not entering a new relationship on the rebound. This will only leave you with unfinished emotions and you will never have closure from your former relationship. **Never begin a new relationship because you are afraid of being on your own or just because you feel the need to be in a relationship.** Form a relationship with someone new because you feel strong and secure on your very own and feel that you are ready to attempt a new romance. Take it one step at a time and keep in mind what your needs and desires are from a person. Watch closely to see if they show signs of the qualities you are looking for. If you notice that he or she is not compatible, then get out of the relationship as soon as possible. Learning from your previous relationships will come in very handy because you will be able to prevent similar situations in the future, leading you to meet the people who fit your description of a perfect partner.

Lastly, remind yourself that love is a wonderful feeling and experience and should not be generalized based on your past experiences. Do not use facts about your previous partner as a way to judge new people in your life. Leave your past behind you and focus on moving ahead. Get to know new people for who they are, not by comparing them to others. Don't focus on what they are not or what they could be. Focus on who they are right now. Once you have observed their personality, values and everything else, trust yourself to make the right decisions without constantly doubting yourself. If you wish to try having a new relationship, then do so. If you do not, however, then do not feel guilty about kindly walking away from the situation. You would be doing both you and the other a person a huge favor and you will save time and emotion. You have nothing to fear or worry about.

Time is the best healer for your heart and mind.

23

Resolving conflict, creating solutions

Many people view conflicts in a relationship as a bad sign. Some believe that couples should not have disagreements. Conflicts are inevitable in intimate relationships, and moreover, they can be seen as excellent opportunities for both personal and relationship growth. From this perspective, conflict is not something to be avoided or minimized but rather something to be embraced as a signal that something needs to change or grow.

We can make anybody understand what we are feeling, but we have to make sure that he or she is sincere. Do not ever interfere with someone's free will and do not ever compel a person to do something, because a relationship is built on trust.

Please talk to your partner when he or she is in a good mood. When a person is in good mood it boosts self-esteem, which is self-love and that makes a person to listen you. A good mood diminishes the ego. The moment the ego is under control, most conflicts will resolve themselves.

However, many people often have areas of conflict that cause repetitive arguments. These problems are very difficult to resolve. If you are experiencing such conflict, you might want to try to use the following method to resolve it. If you are unable to successfully resolve the problem using these tools though, it probably means that the issue is a deeper one and requires professional help such as couple's therapy.

To resolve an ongoing conflict:

1. Identify the area of conflict as specifically as possible. You cannot solve a conflict that is vaguely defined.

2. Using something called a healthy and constructive communication exercise, take turns stating your feelings and thoughts on the issue.

   • Take as long as needed for each of you to fully state your position. Make sure that you don't stop talking until you feel that your partner has really heard you.

   • Just doing this communication exercise sometimes resolves a conflict, though not always.

   • Do not go on to the next step until both of you feel heard by the other one.

3. Brainstorm at least six possible solutions, preferably more.

   • Be creative.

   • Don't worry about being practical; instead, focus on generating as many solutions as possible.

   • Write down all the solutions.

4. Go through the list of solutions together and pick one that you can both agree to try.

   • There may be one obvious solution that you both agree on.

   • You may both have to compromise somewhat to agree on one solution to try.

- Remember that no solution is carved in stone! This is an experiment for a limited period of time that will be evaluated and changed if it does not meet both partners' needs.

5. State the experimental solution as specifically as possible. Write it down if you like.

   - Make sure that nothing will interfere with the solution review.

   - Use the healthy and constructive communication exercise to review how it's going for each of you.

   - Decide if you want to continue implementing the solution

   - If you don't like the solution, modify or enhance it if possible. If that's not possible, start over at the beginning of this exercise.

Conclusion

As you have seen, reflection, meditation and contemplation can bring you success in all of your personal encounters. By understanding our own needs and wants and acknowledging others' perspectives and perceptions, we can employ our new-found awareness to enriching the relationships we have and those we have yet to make. Relationships can be magical, but this magic is the result of the effort two people put into maintaining the harmony between them. Best wishes.

PART IV
RELATIONSHIP TIPS

50 Relationship Tips

1. Relationships need quality time instead of quantity time. Arrange at least fifteen minutes a day and at least one day a month, when you the two of you spend time together exclusively.

2. Tell and show your partner how much you need him or her whenever you have the chance. Create a comfort level.

3. Encourage him or her to listen to you by showing appreciation when he/she does. At the same time, show interest when he or she talks to you.

4. Do not wait for a spontaneous compliment. Say something good about yourself and ask for his or her agreement.

5. Learn to do the one thing that is most likely to restore good feelings in your relationship that may be as simple as giving your partner a genuine, loving and approving smile.

6. Hidden resentments poison a relationship. If something is bothering you, say it. Express your problem and then ask him or her to help you find the answer.

7. People who have a big social network are usually more selective because they may feel they have the most people to choose from. Consider the value other people put on relationships.

8. Physically attractive people without social networking skills are worse off than average looking people with superior social networking skills. Confidence and communication can conquer.

9. People who think they are attractive are more resistant to love and are likely to be more selective. Don't limit yourself.

10. People with low self-esteem or low confidence are more susceptible to love. Unfortunately, this is usually for the wrong reasons.

11. People who are surrounded by eligible and attractive potential partners may stay less committed. Find a partner who shares your goals.

12. Picky people will have a harder time finding their soul mates than average people. Everyone has flaws; sometimes you must make concessions.

13. Money is one of the root causes of conflict. Tackle this obstacle together.

14. Remember that boredom typically covers up anger. If you feel bored with your partner, ask yourself what you're angry about. Try to explore the relationship for causes of this anger so you know what to work on.

15. Be aware that men generally feel overwhelmed by emotion more than women do. If he is angry or tearful, give him some time to himself. This will help get his balance back and make him more able to interact positively with you.

16. Learn how to argue well. The trick is to never say anything that you would not want to hear said to you.

17. Research suggests you need five positive experiences to erase the memory of one negative experience. So give five kind words for each ugly comment.

18. Learn how to negotiate. Each of you states what you want, and then both of you work together to find a way forward.

19. Accept the things that won't change. Some characteristics about your partner are there for life and you have to face that.

20. Learn to forgive. If you know you will never forgive your partner over something important, then give both parties a break and start again—with someone else.

21. Know when to leave. If your life aims are incompatible, or if there is consistently more pain than pleasure, walk out before the relationship destroys you.

22. Plan a Surprise. Keep changing your gifts and your way of giving gifts. Explore various ways. It does not need to be expensive, but it does have to be special. Sometimes the best gifts are the ones that come from the heart and not from the wallet.

23. Use pull and push techniques: This means that you should not always show your complete love and affection. Give the relationship some space and explore the different possibilities. Too much affection has the ability to spoil a relationship.

24. Fun is Important: If you survey couples that have stayed together for years and years and ask them what helped them stay together, most will say that they take pleasure in each other. It is human nature. You stay if you are happy. Learn how to make your own

relationship fun, so both you and your partner enjoy it for years to come.

25. Do not ever make decisions under pressure. Lasting commitment is one you can both strongly believe in. This can only be done after having taken your time to consider it fully.

26. Do not allow name calling in your arguments. If your partner starts calling you names, take a time out and agree to discuss the issue again later.

27. If you find your self-control slipping, count to fifteen or take a break. The aim is to resolve the situation.

28. Use unconditional love to make him or her understand you.

29. You need to have many relationships to be healthy. Remember that your partner is not the only person in your life. Work with your partner to work out concerns. At the same time however, don't do that at the expense of everything else in your life.

30. We often get hurt in an argument because we take every statement as a personal attack even if the comment was not meant that way. Please see things objectively. If you feel that a situation is very hot, call for a break and come back to talk again later.

31. Do you know that intelligent people will find intelligence more attractive in others than those who are not? Likewise, people who do not like themselves will be attracted to others who do not like themselves. Remember that we bring people into our lives who mirror us, both positively and negatively.

32. Similarity in attitudes about social roles explains why some opposites appear to attract each other.

33. Analyze each other to see what makes you truly unique. When you really get to know someone and accept him or her despite his or her flaws, true love sets in.

34. Learn their interests: Older people usually have interests that they have set aside because they did not have the time or ability to pursue them. Help them rekindle those interests. Do this by taking them to shows, buying them equipment, or helping them enroll in classes. By sharing in their interests, you help validate that they still can learn and grow, and be interesting to others.

35. Do not compare others to your partner. Each person has his or her own unique qualities. Instead, discover and balance one another's strengths and weaknesses. Each person should be respected for being an individual.

36. Remember that there is huge difference between meeting in person, talking on the phone, communicating through mail, and Internet chatting. Whenever you get into a problem, please talk to that person directly. Some people are very nervous when making that first contact, and might not express themselves very well.

37. Love is freedom! If you love someone and he or she wants to leave you, let that person go. If he or she comes back to you later and that is what you want, then enjoy that company, but only for the period of time that you both enjoy being together.

38. In relationships the most beautiful satisfaction, joy and love are experienced when there is full freedom, without any fear and addiction.

39. To influence somebody, develop into the kind of a person that they will enjoy being with. Be a good listener if that is all they would like

you to be for now. Do not give them your opinion or advice unless they ask you for it. You could carefully ask them for permission to share with them what is in your heart or on your mind. If they do not want to hear it, then they would not pay attention to your wisdom anyway, especially if you try to force it on them. Do everything possible not to awaken their resistance to what you say or to your presence.

40. A person values nothing more than his or her freedom. To survive, we may temporarily go along with some limitation on our freedom, but only for a time, until we can attain as much freedom as possible. You must learn to respect one another's need for freedom, and not attempt to control it.

41. Each one of us claims a certain amount of space for ourselves. We protect it and don't let any unauthorized people to go over its borders. For instance, you let your loved ones come closer to you than you let a stranger. Establish these boundaries to avoid conflict.

42. Do not cross someone's border if you where not given that privilege, even if he crosses yours. Be gentle and nice but do not let him into your space any more than he lets you into his. Do not let anyone trample you under his or her feet. When you value his and your freedom equally, he will have to choose to value your freedom if he is to enjoy your fellowship. Of course, if you have nothing of value for him then there is nothing you can do.

43. When your partner comes home after being away for some time, make sure that you meet him or her at the door with a loving gesture—whatever way is appropriate in your culture. Treat them as the most important event in your present life.

44. Total love means total freedom. We should allow everyone to be able to do anything they want. That is how God loves. God allows everyone to do anything they want. Conversely, we need to accept the consequences of our choices.

45. Consequences are one's own experience when something does not work. That is, it did not produce an intended result. Learn from this.

46. Love lets go. That which you call need, and which you often confuse with love, does the opposite. Need holds on. This is the way you can tell the difference between love and need. Love lets go; need holds on.

47. Remember that choices are not restrictions. Do not call the choices you have made restrictions. Lovingly provide your offspring and all your loved ones with all the information you may have to help them make good choices, those most likely to lead to happiness.

48. Offer that which you have come to understand. At the same time do not seek to impose your ideas, your rules, or your choices upon another. Do not withhold your love should another make choices you would not make. Indeed, if you believe their choices to have been poor ones, that is precisely the time to show your love.

49. Be a medium to channel your partner's anger or resentment. If your partner needs to vent their emotions, give them a safe and comfortable place to do so.

50. If you really like someone, don't shower them with too much affection. Use moderation. Find a way to exhibit your self-esteem, make them laugh and not seem too keen. You need to become a Challenge to them, not a pushover.

Appendix A

Other resources in relationship therapy

Energy psychology techniques like Emotional Freedom Technique (EFT) and Thought Field Therapy (TFT) can help us to melt the negative feelings of injury, disgrace, and insufficiency that your inner enemy can always extract. We must plant a seed of positive energy into our inner thoughts in order to dismantle the enemy.

Emotional Field Technology:

EFT Centers on the deep effects of the body's subtle energies using the theory that the cause of all negative emotions is a disruption in the body's energy system. Accordingly, EFT is an emotional form of acupuncture except without any needles. Instead, professionals tap with the fingertips to stimulate certain meridian energy points while the client is "tuned in" to the problem.

Though Field therapy:

Thought Field Therapy (TFT) is the procedure that provides a code to nature's healing system, when applied to problems, TFT addresses a problem's fundamental causes, balancing the body's energy system and allowing you to eliminate most negative emotions within minutes. This code is elicited through TFT's unique assessment procedures.

Appendix B

Helpful hints in reading a potential partner's intentions

How to come to a conclusion that one has fallen love with you:

- He or she keeps on trying to talk to you and spend time with you.

- They come up with an interesting question regarding their life plan.

- The eyes are the key to identifying whether a person loves somebody. No one can keep their love from showing through their eyes.

- One can feel love in silence, through the eyes, and through touch.

Signal Techniques:

Red: No way
Amber: Neutral
Green: Go ahead

If you want to find out if a person is interested in you, ask open-ended questions about the person he or she wants to settle down with. Listen to the answers carefully.

If they say a person like you or with qualities like yours...**Green**

If they say let's not talk about this now...**Amber**

If they say I am not interested in this topic...**Red**

APPENDIX C

Regarding men and women

Common male and female thoughts (Common):

Men and women are unable to ever completely be regarded as the same. They possess different qualities and natures, which shape their perspectives. Below are some patterns that can be useful in understanding the motivations of someone of the opposite sex. These are in no way concrete, merely representative of some common generalities.

Men:

- Want to achieve success and accomplishment. Men want to prove themselves, which is a means of gaining confidence. They work to prove their power, perseverance, and strength, often through competition. They rarely ask for suggestions, even if they need them because this can be interpreted as a lack of control/power

- Love, feelings, and affections are often secondary for men. They are more goal-oriented.

- Men are often more aggressive, combative, territorial, logical, analytical, and rational than women.

- Men have a much more difficult time relating to their own feelings and may feel very threatened by the expression of feelings in their presence.

- Men are often more at ease with exhibiting their angry emotions than women.

- Men tend to be more practical in approaching problem solving; women are feeling-oriented in addition to being functional.

- Men feel devastated by failure and financial setbacks; they tend to obsess about money much more than women. They hate to ask for information because it shows weakness.

Women:

- Women tend to value love, communication, affection, beauty and relationships.

- A women's image of self is often defined through their feelings. This can be influenced by the quality of their relationships with men.

- Their strengths often lie in supporting, nurturing, loving, and helping others. They experience fulfillment through sharing and relating.

- They place more importance upon personal expression, dress, presentation, communication and feelings.

- Talking, sharing, coming to know about others and relating is often how a woman feels good about herself.

- Women usually don't want to be alone. They want somebody to love them and they need love and affection.

- For women, offering help is not a sign of weakness, but a sign of strength and caring. They set examples for calm and cool.

- When a female does not have a person to love she often feels sad. Women tend to live for others and whenever they give deep affection, they feel real meditation.

- Women are often more intuitive, holistic, creative, and integrative than men. Women are in touch with a much wider range of feelings than men, and the intensity of those feelings is usually much greater for women than men.

How to work out differences:

- When women are upset, it may not the best time to offer solutions. It may be more appropriate in the future when she is calmer. For the most part, she just wants to feel heard and understood at the time.

- A man appreciates advice and criticism when it is requested. Men want to make improvements when they feel they are being approached as a solution to a problem rather than the problem itself.

- Men have great needs for status and independence (emphasis on separate and different); women have needs for intimacy and connection (emphasis on close and same).

- Women need to receive caring, understanding, respect, devotion, validation, and reassurance.

- Women are motivated when they feel special or cherished.

- Men need to receive trust, acceptance, appreciation, admiration, approval, and encouragement.

- Men are motivated when they feel needed. A man's deepest fear is that he is not good enough or not competent enough, though he may never express this.

Finally:

The differences between men and women are just that—different. They are not better or worse. Do not judge the differences. Do not try to change the differences. Do not try to make them go away. Individual differences exist, but we all have some of these qualities. To get along, you MUST accept, expect and respect these differences. Be sure to remember these differences when communicating about anything important, when expressing care and concern, and when solving conflicts.

About the Author

Saha Nathan is the author of three best-selling books in India, one of the successful books called *Customer Relationship Management—A Step By Step Approach* has been included in more than 25 university syllabi in India. **Saha Nathan** has over ten years of experience in relationship management, traveling extensively to conduct seminars on building and strengthening relationships. He holds a Bachelor of Engineering degree and an MBA from Madurai University, India, and is currently pursuing his PH.D. in Relationship Management at Anna University in India. Saha currently lives in Seattle, Washington, and can be contacted at: www.sahasworld.com.

978-0-595-35449-8
0-595-35449-1